Jeden Tag besser

Englisch

Test- und Übungsheft

5. Klasse

W0408615

Cornelsen
SCRIPTOR

Lernplan von ____________________

Wortarten: Nomen	Bearbeitet am	☹ 😐 ☺	↺ ✓
Singular und Plural 4		◯	
Paarwörter 6		◯	
Genitiv-s / Plural-s 8		◯	
s-Genitiv / of-Genitiv 10		◯	
Plural-s / Genitiv-s / 3.-Person-Singular-s 12		◯	
Wortarten: Pronomen und Mengenangaben	**Bearbeitet am**	☹ 😐 ☺	↺ ✓
Personalpronomen 14		◯	
Possessivbegleiter 16		◯	
Mengenangaben 18		◯	
Wortarten: Präpositionen und Zahlen	**Bearbeitet am**	☹ 😐 ☺	↺ ✓
Präpositionen des Ortes (1) 20		◯	
Präpositionen des Ortes (2) 22		◯	
Datumsangaben und Ordnungszahlen (1) 24		◯	
Datumsangaben und Ordnungszahlen (2) 26		◯	

Singular und Plural

1 **Hier siehst du Beispiele für die Pluralbildung im Englischen. Schreibe unter jedes Beispiel zwei weitere Nomen, die ihren Plural genauso bilden.**

Tipp: Wenn dir keine Nomen einfallen, schlag in deinem Schulbuch oder in einem Wörterbuch nach!

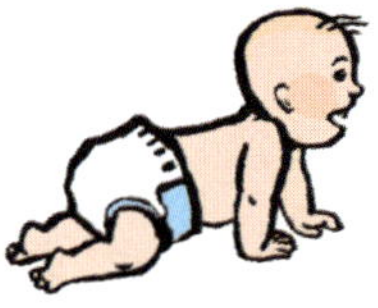

Singular – Einzahl	**Plural – Mehrzahl**
a baby	two babies
______________	______________
______________	______________
a knife	two knives
______________	______________
______________	______________
a sandwich	two sandwiches
______________	______________
______________	______________

__ 12

Manche englischen Nomen haben im Singular und im Plural dieselbe Form. Andere bilden den Plural mit einer Sonderform, z. B.: *child – children.*

2 **Schreibe hier ein Nomen auf, das seinen Plural ganz anders bildet als die Nomen aus Aufgabe 1.**

______________ ______________

__ 2

3 Setze die Pluralformen der Nomen ein, die du auf den Bildern siehst.

This is my classroom. There are twelve *tables*  and twenty-four

__________  in my classroom. In it there are three

__________ . There are six __________ 

and eight __________ . We have got two __________ .

You can write on them. I can see four __________ .

In one of the school bags there are two __________ .

On the walls there are two __________  of Great Britain.

Through one of the two __________  I can see

two __________  in the street.

There are five __________ , three __________ 

and four __________  at the bus stop. Eight __________ 

and seven __________  are playing football in the park.

There are fifteen __________  in front of the school. 16

30–25 Punkte | 24–16 Punkte | 15–0 Punkte | Gesamtpunktzahl

Paarwörter

Manche Dinge bestehen aus zwei gleichen Teilen. Für diese Dinge verwendet man im Englischen ein Paarwort (*pair noun*). Paarworte stehen im Plural. Wenn man ein Paarwort mit einem Verb verbindet, steht auch das Verb im Plural.

Ein Beispiel: *I like his new trousers. They are very nice.*

1 Schreibe jeweils das richtige Paarwort unter die Bilder.

glasses sunglasses scissors jeans

trousers shorts pyjamas scales

1 ______________

2 ______________

3 ______________

4 ______________

5 ______________

6 ______________

7 ______________

8 ______________

__ | 8

2 **Ergänze in den folgenden Sätzen die richtige Form des Verbs in Klammern.**

Angela's new glasses ______ (to be) great. I really like them.

Where ______ (to be) my black trousers? I can't find them.

Damian's jeans ______ (to look) good on him.

Emma's pyjamas ______ (to be) white with red stripes. | 4

Wenn man Paarwörter zählen will, muss man die Mengenangabe *pair of* benutzen: *I have got one pair of sunglasses and two pairs of glasses.*

3 **Schreibe die Zahlen und die richtigen Mengenangaben in die Lücken.**

There are (3) ______ scissors in the classroom.

Mrs Nolan has got (1) ______ scissors.

Who has got the other (2) ______ scissors?

How many ______ trousers does Kelly have? She has got (5) ______ trousers and (4) ______ jeans. But she has only got (1) ______ shorts.

There are (2) ______ scales on the table.

(1)______ scales is black.

The other______ scales is golden.

pro richtig geschriebener Zahl 1 Punkt | 8
pro richtiger Mengenangabe zum Paarwort 1 Punkt | 10

30–25 Punkte

24–15 Punkte

14–10 Punkte

Gesamtpunktzahl

Genitiv-s / Plural-s

1 **Die Sachen auf der Wäscheleine gehören Jane. Fülle die Lücken in den folgenden Sätzen.**

On the line, there are three ____________ and two

____________ and four ____________.

Are they Tom's clothes? No, they are ____________ clothes.

4

Es gibt zwei verschiedene Sorten von angehängtem *-s*:
Das eine *-s* zeigt den Plural an, z. B.: *one T-shirt – three T-shirts.*
Das andere *-s* zeigt, wozu etwas gehört oder wem etwas gehört, z. B.:
This is Emma's skirt. oder *My father's job is interesting.* oder
The girls' team wins.

Mehrzahl	Besitzer
one T-shirt two T-shirts	Jane's T-shirt the Jacksons' T-shirts
s anhängen	**erst ein Apostroph (= '), dann ein s anhängen; hat das Nomen aber schon ein Mehrzahl-s am Ende, wird nur ein Apostroph angehängt (girls' team)**

2 **Unterstreiche im folgenden Text alle Wörter in der Mehrzahl.** 16

3 **Umkreise dann alle Wörter, die einen oder mehrere Besitzer anzeigen.** 15

The children are on a school trip. The children's bags are in the bus. Now the girls are in their rooms. They are sitting on their beds. The girls' beds are very nice. But there is something wrong with Jane's bed. She can't sit on it. "Where are my new tennis shoes?" Helen asks. Helen's new tennis shoes are in Jane's bed. Where is Mr Johnson, the pupils' teacher? The door to Mr Johnson's room is open, but he isn't in. His things, his pullovers, T-shirts, jeans and shoes are still in his bag. Why is Mr Johnson not in his room? He is in the boys' room. The boys' room is on the first floor. One of the boys is very angry. Why?

4 **Die Mädchen haben den Jungen auf der Klassenfahrt einen Streich gespielt und ihre Sachen versteckt. Schreibe auf, wessen Sachen sich wo befinden.**

Patrick's ______________ are under ______________ bed.

______________ are on Patrick's bed. Paul's socks are in

______________ wardrobe. ______________ jeans are behind the door of the

boys' room. Bob's pullover is under ______________ wardrobe.

______________ wardrobe is closed. But what is hanging on

______________ wardrobe? It is ______________ anorak. 9

44–38 Punkte | 37–23 Punkte | 22–0 Punkte | Gesamtpunktzahl

s-Genitiv / of-Genitiv

1 Wem gehören die Geschenke? Folge den Linien mit den Augen oder mit einem Stift. Ergänze dann die Sätze.

1. The CD is *Adam's present*.
2. Mary's present is the ______________________________.
3. ____ the book.
4. The football ____.
5. Ralph's present ____.
6. ____ the jigsaw puzzle.
7. ____ the pullover.

6

Den s-Genitiv hast du schon kennengelernt, z. B.: *my sister's book* (Singular) oder *the boys' shirts* (Plural). Geht es bei der Angabe des Besitzers oder besser der Zugehörigkeit nicht um lebende Wesen, wird der Genitiv mit *of* gebildet, z. B.: *This is the end of the game. Inspector Exley is walking down the middle of the road.*

2 **Schau dir die Geschenke und ihre Preisschilder noch einmal an. Bilde nun mit den Satzteilen in Klammern ganze Sätze. Schreibe auch die fehlenden Angaben auf, z. B. den Preis oder das Geschenk.**

Tipp: In dieser Übung kommen beide Genitiv-Formen vor.

1. (price / to be / £ 11.50) *£ 11.50 is the price of the football.*
   The price of the football is £ 11.50.
2. (price / to be / £3.75) ______
3. (price / Ralph / present / to be) ______
4. (price / CD / to be) ______
5. (price / to be / £ 4.50) ______
6. (price / pullover / to be) ______
7. (price / Mary / present / to be) ______

☐ 12

☐ 18 – 14 Punkte | 13 – 9 Punkte | 8 – 0 Punkte | ☐ Gesamtpunktzahl

Plural-s / Genitiv-s / 3.-Person-Singular-s

1 **Schau dir das Schaufenster des Spielwarengeschäftes genau an und schreibe auf, was du sehen kannst. Gib auch die Anzahl der Gegenstände an.**

Tipp: Wörter, die du nicht kennst, findest du vielleicht am Ende der Seite.

I can see two ______________________________

____

____

____

____

____

____

chessboard Schachbrett – *kite* (ausgesprochen: keit) Drachen – *doll* Puppe – *model plane* Modellflugzeug – *model train* Modelleisenbahn – *knight* Ritter – *toy car* Spielzeugauto

8

2 **Was wünschen sich die Kinder zum Geburtstag? Schreibe ganze Sätze auf.**

Brenda wants ....

Kevin ....

....

.... [ ] 4

3 **Die Eltern der Kinder haben andere Ideen. Was wollen sie ihren Kindern kaufen? Schreibe ganze Sätze auf.**

Brenda's father wants to buy a doll for Brenda.

Kevin's mother ....

....

....

.... [ ] 4

[ ] 16–13 Punkte 12–9 Punkte 8–0 Punkte [ ] Gesamtpunktzahl

Personalpronomen

Personalpronomen (*personal pronouns*) können Subjekt oder Objekt eines Satzes sein. Ein Beispiel: ***I see you and you see me.***

Subjekt	Objekt
I	me
you	you
he	him
she	her

Subjekt	Objekt
we	us
you	you
they	them

1 Heute trifft sich die Basketball-Schulmannschaft. Mr Howard, der Trainer, macht eine Liste, wer zum Training gekommen ist.
Lies, wie Mr Howard mit seiner Mannschaft die Liste durchgeht. Trage die Personalpronomen in die Lücken ein. Die Liste der *personal pronouns* hilft dir dabei.

Mr Howard: "What class are ______ in, John?"

John: "__________ am in class 1A." Mr Howard: "Peter and Mary are on the list. But __________ are not here today."

Susan: "Peter is at home. __________ know that __________ is ill. But Mary? __________ don't know where __________ is."

Mr Howard: "What class are they in?"

Susan: "__________ are both in my class. __________ are all in class 1C."

Mr Howard: "And what about __________, Sam and Sally?"

Sam and Sally: "__________ are in class 1C, too."

Mr Howard: "What about Julia? Where is __________?"

Sam and Sally: "We always see __________ on the bus. She and Colin often play basketball with __________ after school."

Mr Howard: "What class are they in?"

John: "Colin? ________ is in the same class as me. Julia is in class 1B."

Mr Howard: "OK. ________ am nearly finished. But Tracy Bond and Tom Taylor are on the list, too. Where are ________? And what class are ________ in?"

Susan: "________ don't know where ________ are but I know what class Tracy is in. ________ is in class 1 B, too."

John: "________ know Tom. ________ is in class 1 A, too. But today ________ is not here. His mum is taking ________ to the dentist at 11.00."

☐ 25

2 **Fülle nun Mr Howards Anwesenheitsliste vollständig aus. Lies dazu noch einmal das Gespräch zwischen Mr Howard und seiner Mannschaft.**

name	**class**	**is there**	**is not there**
Sam Barns		**X**	
Tracy Bond			
Colin Johnson			
Julia Johnson			**X**
Peter Martin			**X**
Mary McKenzie			
Susan Patterson			
Tom Taylor			
John Wilson	**1 A**	**X**	
Sally Winters	**1 C**		

☐ 14

☐ 39–31 Punkte 30–20 Punkte 19–0 Punkte ☐ Gesamtpunktzahl

Possessivbegleiter

Possessivbegleiter* (*possessive adjectives* oder *possessive determiners*) sagen dir, wem etwas gehört.

I	my
you	your
he	his
she	her
it	its

we	our
you	your
they	their

1 **Schau dir die Bilder an. Was gehört wem?**
Ergänze in den Sätzen auf der nächsten Seite die Possessivbegleiter.

*Die deutschen Begriffe „Possessivbegleiter", „besitzanzeigender Begleiter" und „Possessivadjektiv" bedeuten dasselbe.

1. "Is that Mary's red bag?" • Peter: "No, __________ bag is black."
2. "Where are Janet's and Peter's rulers?" • Paul: "__________ rulers are under the red bag."
3. "What colour is Paul's pencil?" • Paul: "__________ pencil is green."
4. "Janet, is that your English book?" • Janet: "No, it's _____ German book."
5. "Janet and Peter, are these your pencils?" • Janet and Peter: "Yes, these are __________ pencils."
6. "Is that __________ jacket, Janet?" • Janet: "No, it's not __________ jacket. I think it's John's."
7. John: "No, it's not __________ jacket. Mary, is that __________ jacket?" Mary: "Oh yes, this is __________ jacket!"
8. John: "Where is __________ apple?" • Janet: "It's next to __________ cap."
9. John: "What colour is __________ cap, Janet?" • Janet: "__________ colour is blue."
10. Paul: "Look, here's a sandwich!" • John: "It's __________ sandwich. You can have it."
11. Peter: "That is Mary's English book." • Paul: "No, it's not __________ English book! It's __________ English book!"
12. "There is one thing left: the red bag. I think it's Janet's bag." Janet: "No it's not __________ bag. It's John's, it's __________ red bag." 19

19–15 Punkte | 14–10 Punkte | 9–0 Punkte | Gesamtpunktzahl

Mengenangaben

Wenn wir nach einer bestimmten Menge fragen, benutzen wir *how many*.
Nach einer unbestimmten Menge fragt man mit *how much*.
How many boys are there in this class? There are 14 boys in this class.
How much cheese do you eat? I eat a lot of cheese.

1 **Oben siehst du die Lebensmittel, die Ben und Jamie kaufen möchten. Trage die Wörter in die folgende Tabelle ein.**

How many?	How much?
bottles of milk	*milk*
sausages	

9

2 **Ben und Jamie unterhalten sich beim Einkaufen. Schreibe in jede Lücke die richtige Mengenangabe – entweder *how much* oder *how many*.**

1. Ben: "__________________ butter have you got in the trolley*?"

   Jamie: "I've got three packets. __________________ packets of butter are there on the list?"

2. Ben: "There are three, that's OK. And there is coffee on the list. __________________ have you got in the trolley?" Jamie: "I've got one pound."

3. Ben: "We need three bottles of milk. __________________ have you got in the trolley?" Jamie: "I've got four bottles." Ben: "Oh, that's not right."

4. Jamie: "Why not? __________________ bottles are on the list?" Ben: "There are only three bottles on the list! And there are sausages on the list, too."

5. Jamie: "__________________ sausages do we need?"

6. Ben: "We need four sausages. __________________ have you got?" Jamie: "I've got four sausages. Is that everything?"

7. Ben: "No, we need tea. But __________________ tea?"

8. Jamie: "I don't know __________________ tea we need." [ ] 9

* *trolley* = Einkaufswagen

3 **Ergänze die folgenden Sätze.**

________________________ orange juice do we need?

________________________ bottles of orange juice do we need? [ ] 2

[ ] 20–16 Punkte | 15–11 Punkte | 10–0 Punkte | [ ] Gesamtpunktzahl

Präpositionen des Ortes (1)

1 In Sarahs Zimmer haben es sich viele Katzen gemütlich gemacht. Trage die fehlenden Präpositionen des Ortes in den Lückentext ein. Streiche die Präpositionen durch, die du schon benutzt hast.

in front of ~~*under*~~ *in* *on* *behind* *under*
behind *on* *in* *against* *on* *next to*

Sarah: "Oh no, there are cats everywhere! There's a cat *under* the sofa and another cat is ____________ the chair, one cat is ____________ the armchair. So many cats! There are cats leaning ____________ the vase, lying ____________ the basket, balancing ____________ the lamp, sitting ____________ the cupboard and ____________ the bookshelf, sleeping ____________ the cupboard, standing ____________ the door, sitting ____________ the TV and standing ____________ the sofa."

11

2 **Sarahs Bruder Jamie findet in seinem Zimmer nichts mehr wieder. Hilf ihm und beantworte seine Fragen.**

1. Where's my new basketball? *Your/The new basketball is on the chair.*
2. Can you see my skateboard? Where are my comics?

____

____

3. My mountain bike is not in the garage. Where is it?

____

4. I want to play the guitar. But I can't find my guitar.

____

5. What about my TV? I can't see it. Where are my old white shoes?

____

____

6. I am looking for some books and for a football. Can you see them?

____

____ [ ] 8

[ ] 19–15 Punkte | 14–10 Punkte | 9–0 Punkte | [ ] Gesamtpunktzahl

Präpositionen des Ortes (2)

1 Schau dir das Bild an und beantworte dann die Fragen. Die Präpositionen unter dem Bild helfen dir dabei. Einige brauchst du mehrmals.

behind *on* *in the middle of* *under* *in front of* *next to*

1. Where is the football?

   The football is on the bench.

2. Where are the woman and the baby?

   ____

3. Where is the boy?

   ____

4. Where is the man on the bike?

   ____

5. Where is the policeman standing?

   ______________________________ *the road.*

6. Where is the postman?

____ *the phone box.*

7. Where is the girl?

____

8. Where is the dog?

____ |__|7|

2 **Bob beschreibt seinen Schulweg.**
Schreibe die passenden Präpositionen in die Lücken. Streiche die Präpositionen durch, die du bereits verwendet hast.

~~*out of*~~ *into* *into* *into* *round* *out* *down* *over*
over *at* *next to* *through* *on*

Bob: "First I go *out of* the house and *i*__________ the garden. I jump __________ the fence. Then I walk __________ the road. I turn left __________ the traffic lights. I go __________ the corner and __________ Green Street. Then I go __________ the supermarket. The supermarket is __________ the bank. I buy a sandwich there and go __________ again. The school is __________ the other side of the park. Sometimes I climb __________ the wall and sometimes I go __________ the gate." |__|12|

|__| 19–15 Punkte 14–10 Punkte 9–0 Punkte |__| Gesamtpunktzahl

Datumsangaben und Ordnungszahlen (1)

So wird ein Datum geschrieben:
July 20th oder *July 20*
20th July oder *20 July*

So wird es gesprochen:
July the twentieth
the twentieth of July

Die Zahlen, mit denen wir etwas aufzählen, nennen wir Ordnungszahlen (*ordinal numbers*): *my first book* = mein erstes Buch oder *my fourth visit* = mein vierter Besuch.

1 Hier siehst du Beckys Terminkalender für den April. Trage darin die fehlenden Ordnungszahlen ein. Schreibe Zahlen oder Wörter, je nachdem, was fehlt.

	April	
1st	first	*April Fool's Day*
2nd	second	*circus in town*
3rd		*Jenny's party*
4th	fourth	*go shopping with Mum*
9th	ninth	*have lunch with Sarah*
10th	tenth	*guitar club*
11th		*Dad's birthday*
	twelfth	*tennis match in London*
	thirteenth	*take Blacky for a walk*
14th		*meet Josh and Hannah*
15th		
16th		*go to the cinema*
18th		*play volleyball at school*
19th		*go for a walk with Ben*
22nd	twenty-second	*Brenda's birthday*
	twenty-third	*swimming pool opens*
24th		*visit Grandpa*

11

2 **Schau dir Beckys Kalender noch einmal genau an.
Beantworte die folgenden Fragen.**

1. When is Jenny's party? *Jenny's party is on 3rd April / April 3rd.*
2. When does Becky play volleyball at school?

   ____

3. When is Brenda's birthday?

   ____

4. Does Becky meet Josh and Hannah on 8th April?

   ____

5. Does the swimming pool open on 21st April?

   ____

6. Does Becky have lunch with Sarah on 8th April?

   ____

7. When does Becky go for a walk with Ben?

   ____

8. Does she go to the cinema on 17th April?

   ____

9. Does Becky visit her Grandpa on 27th April?

   ____

10. When is April Fool's Day?

   ____

☐ | 9

☐ 20–16 Punkte 15–11 Punkte 10–0 Punkte ☐ Gesamtpunktzahl

Datumsangaben und Ordnungszahlen (2)

1 **Dana hat eine Geburtstagsliste für den Monat Mai angelegt, damit sie niemanden vergisst. Schau dir Danas Liste an und schreibe zu jedem Geburtstag einen Satz auf. Schreibe die Altersangaben aus.**

1st	*Susan 15 tomorrow!*	→ *buy a CD for her*
3rd	*Jennifer 12 today*	→ *go to the cinema with her*
12th	*Me! 12 today!*	→ *have a party*
19th	*Daddy 51 tomorrow*	→ *buy a toy car for him*
22nd	*little brother Tommy 8 tomorrow*	→ *make a cake for him*
24th		→ *write and send Janet a birthday card*
25th	*big sister Vic 22 today*	→ *call* her in London*
28th	*Janet 13 today*	
31st	*John 9 today*	→ *take him to the zoo*

* *to call* = anrufen

On May 2nd it's Susan's fifteenth birthday.

On ______________________ *Jennifer's* ________________ *birthday.*

______________________________ *it's my* ________________________________

____

____

____

______________________________ *Janet's* ________________________________

____

7

2 **Schau dir Danas Liste noch einmal an und schreibe auf, was Dana im Mai erledigt.**

On May 1st Dana buys a CD for Susan.

On ______________ *Dana* ______________________ *with Jennifer.*

____

____

____

____

____

____

____ /7

14–12 Punkte | 11–8 Punkte | 7–0 Punkte | Gesamtpunktzahl

to be im *simple present*

lange Form	kurze Form
I am	I’m
you are	you’re
he / she / it is	he’s / she’s / it’s

lange Form	kurze Form
we are	we’re
you are	you’re
they are	they’re

Lösungen

★ Aufgaben mit höherem Schwierigkeitsgrad

Seite 4

1 Einige Beispiele:

a baby	**two babies**
a copy, a family, a pony, a lady	two copies, two families, two ponies, two ladies
a knife	**two knives**
a shelf, a life, a wolf, a half	two shelves, two lives, two wolves, two halves
a sandwich	**two sandwiches**
a dish, a match, a bush, a glass	two dishes, two matches, two bushes, two glasses

2 Beispiele für ganz andere Pluralformen: a sheep – two sheep, a mouse – two mice, a tooth – two teeth, a man – two men, a woman – two women

Seite 5

3 chairs, cupboards, books, glasses, blackboards, school bags, sandwiches, maps, windows, policemen, children, men, women, boys, girls, bicycles

Seite 6

1 Bild 1: glasses; Bild 2: shorts;
Bild 3: scissors; Bild 4: trousers;
Bild 5: sunglasses; Bild 6: scales;
Bild 7: jeans; Bild 8: pyjamas

Seite 7

2 are, are, look, are

3★ three pairs of, one pair of, two pairs of, pairs of, five pairs of, four pairs of, one pair of, two pairs of, One pair of, pair of

Seite 8

1 T-shirts, pairs of trousers, socks, Jane's

Seite 9

2 + 3
The children are on a school trip. The children's bags are in the bus. Now the girls are in their rooms. They are sitting on their beds. The girls' beds are very nice. But there is something wrong with Jane's bed. She can't sit on it. "Where are my new tennis shoes?" Helen asks. Helen's new tennis shoes are in Jane's bed. Where is Mr Johnson, the pupils' teacher? The door to Mr Johnson's room is open, but he isn't in. His things, his pullovers, T-shirts, jeans and shoes are still in his bag. Why is Mr Johnson not in his room? He is in the boys' room. The boys' room is on the first floor. One of the boys is very angry. Why?

4 shoes, Kevin's, Tim's T-shirts, Tim's, Bob's, Kevin's, Bob's, John's, Patrick's

Seite 10

1
2. Mary's present is the box of sweets.
3. Tom's present is the book.
4. The football is Colin's present.
5. Ralph's present is the pencil case.
6. Susan's present is the jigsaw puzzle.
7. Linda's present is the pullover.

Seite 11

2
2. £3.75 is the price of the jigsaw puzzle / The price of the jigsaw puzzle is £3.75.
3. The price of Ralph's present is £3.10. / £3.10 is the price of Ralph's present.

Lösungen

4. The price of the CD is £12. / £12 is the price of the CD.
5. The price of the book is £4.50. / £4.50 is the price of the book.
6. The price of the pullover is £ 10. / £10 is the price of the pullover.
7. The price of Mary's present is £2.50. / £2.50 is the price of Mary's present.

Seite 12

1 I can see two chessboards, two dolls, three model planes, three teddy bears/ teddies, two kites, four toy cars, five knights on horses and two model trains.

Seite 13

2 Brenda wants a skateboard.
Kevin wants a kite.
Julia wants a football.
Patrick wants a mountain bike.

3 Kevin's mother wants to buy two books for Kevin.
Kevin's father wants to buy a computer for Kevin.
Julia's mother wants to buy three CDs for Julia.
Patrick's father wants to buy toy cars for Patrick.

Seite 14

1 you – I – they – I – he – I – she – They – We – you – We – she – her – us – He – I – they – they – I – they – She – I – He – he – him

Seite 15

2

name	class	is there	is not there
Sam Barns	1 C	X	
Tracy Bond	1 B		X
Colin Johnson	1 A		X
Julia Johnson	1 B		X
Peter Martin	1 C		X
Mary McKenzie	1 C		X
Susan Patterson	1 C	X	
Tom Taylor	1 A		X
John Wilson	1 A	X	
Sally Winters	1 C	X	

Seite 16 / 17

1 1. her; 2. Their; 3. My; 4. my; 5. our; 6. your, my; 7. my, your, my; 8. my, my; 9. your, Its; 10. my; 11. her, my; 12. my, his

Seite 18

1

How many?	How much?
bottles of milk	milk
sausages	cheese
melons	bread
apples	coffee
carrots	tea
tomatoes	butter

Seite 19

2 1. How much, How many; 2. How much; 3. How many; 4. How many; 5. How many; 6. How many; 7. how much; 8. how much

3 How much orange juice do we need?
How many bottles of orange juice do we need?

Lösungen

Seite 20

① on the chair, behind the armchair, against the vase, in the basket, on the lamp, in the cupboard, on the bookshelf, under the cupboard, behind the door, in front of the TV, next to the sofa

Seite 21

②★ 2. Your/The skateboard is on the bed. Your/The comics are on the table.
3. Your/The mountain bike is behind the door.
4. Your/The guitar is under the bed.
5. Your/The TV is under the table. Your/The old white shoes are in front of the bed.
6. Your/The books are on the floor. Your/The football is on the bed.

Seite 22

①
2. The woman and the baby/They are next to the bus stop.
3. The boy/He is in front of the supermarket.
4. The man on the bike/He is behind the red bus.
5. The policeman/He is standing in the middle of the road.
6. The postman/He is next to the phone box.
7. The girl/She is in front of the post office.
8. The dog is under the tree.

Seite 23

② into the garden, over the fence, down the road, at the traffic lights, round the corner, into Green Street, into the supermarket, next to the bank, out again, on the other side of the park, over the wall, through the gate

Seite 24

① 3rd – third, 11th – eleventh, 12th – twelfth, 13th – thirteenth, fourteenth, fifteenth, sixteenth, eighteenth, nineteenth, 23rd – twenty-third, 24th – twenty-fourth

Seite 25

②
2. Becky plays volleyball at school on 18th April/April 18th.
3. Brenda's birthday is on 22nd April/April 22nd.
4. No, Becky meets Josh and Hannah on 14th April/April 14th.
5. No, the swimming pool opens on 23rd April/April 23rd.
6. No, Becky has lunch with Sarah on 9th April/April 9th.
7. Becky goes for a walk with Ben on 19th April/April 19th.
8. No, she goes to the cinema on 16th April/April 16th.
9. No, Becky visits her Grandpa on 24th April/April 24th.
10. April Fool's Day is on 1st April/April 1st.

Lösungen

Seite 26

1 On May 3rd it's Jennifer's twelfth birthday.
On May 12th it's my twelfth birthday.
On May 20th it's Daddy's/Dad's fifty-first birthday.
On May 23rd it's my little brother Tommy's eighth birthday.
On May 25th it's my big sister Vic's twenty-second birthday.
On May 28th it's Janet's thirteenth birthday.
On May 31st it's John's ninth birthday.

Seite 27

2★ On May 3rd Dana goes to the cinema with Jennifer.
On May 12th Dana has a party.
On May 19th Dana buys a toy car for her father/Dad/Daddy.
On May 22nd Dana makes a cake for her little brother Tommy.
On May 24th Dana writes and sends Janet a birthday card.
On May 25th Dana calls her big sister Vic in London.
On May 31st Dana takes John to the zoo.

Seite 37

1 1. are, are; 2. are, is, is, are; 3. is; 4. is; 5. are; 6. am, is

2 1. are; 2. Is, is, is; 3. Is, is, is; 4. is, is, are; 5. are; 6. is, is

Seite 38

1

to go	swimming, ice-skating, fishing
to make	music, model planes
to collect	action figures, baseball cards, (model planes), (magazines), (comics)
to play	football, the guitar, computer games
to listen to	the radio, (music)
to read	magazines, a book, comics
to watch	TV

Seite 39

2★ In the evening he always watches TV. At the weekend he sometimes goes fishing with his friends. He makes model planes, too.
Daniel and Emma sometimes do things together. They collect action figures and play computer games. In the evening they often listen to music or read a book.
Emma always plays hockey in the afternoon. She plays the guitar, too. On Sundays she often goes swimming with her friend Sandra. She never plays football. She hates it.

Seite 40

1 She doesn't play table tennis in the park.
She doesn't go to the sports club.
She doesn't work in the garden.
She doesn't read a magazine.
Dylan doesn't go swimming.
He doesn't go fishing in the river.
He doesn't ride his bike.
He doesn't play football.
He doesn't visit Grandma.

Seite 41

2 My sister Lisa is not in the garden. She and my mother do not like gardening. My brother Alan is not on a bike ride. On Sundays I do not go fishing with my friend Bob. I do not often go fishing. The weather is not fine.
Lisa does not take our dog for a walk

every afternoon. We do not have a lot to do today.

Seite 42 / 43

1
2. Are the traffic lights red for the bus every morning at eight o'clock?
3. Does the cat run after the dog every morning?
4. Who talks to reckless drivers every morning?
5. Does the postman stop at number 34? But he always stops at number 32.
6. Do the boys go to school on their rollerblades?
7. Does bus number 4 go to Portobello? It goes to Leith.
8. Does the girl look in the window of the toy shop every morning? She looks in the window of the pet shop every morning.

Seite 44 / 45

1
2. Why does Jack buy chocolate bars? He buys chocolate bars because he is hungry.
3. Where does Vicky buy magazines? She buys magazines at the kiosk.
4. What do Julia and Tim buy? They buy bread and ten eggs.
5. What does Mrs Solomon buy? She buys a packet of cornflakes and two bottles of milk.
6. Why do Ben and Jamie buy a comic? They buy a comic because they want to read it.
7. What does Mr Smart buy? He buys a book.
8. When does Lisa buy a new T-shirt? She buys a new T-shirt on Monday.
9. Where does Hannah buy three bottles of apple juice? She buys three bottles of apple juice at the supermarket.
10. When does Mr Pott buy a new bicycle? He buys a new bicycle on Saturday.

Seite 46

1 I'm – you're – I'm – Let's – That's – it's – haven't – Don't – don't – here's – He's – let's – It's – that's – don't

Seite 47

2 Text B ist richtig.

3 My parents and I don't like that snack-bar because the waiter's not very friendly. He's old and he's got a dog called Annie. She's black and she's got a very big mouth. My father doesn't want me to play with her. He's not happy with dogs.

Seite 48 / 49

1★
2. Does Mike put on his school uniform at 7.15 a.m.? Yes, he puts on his school uniform at 7.15 a.m.
3. Mike leaves the house at 8.30 a.m.
4. Does school start at 8.00 a.m.? No, school starts at 9.00 a.m.
5. Mike doesn't have lunch at 1.00 p.m.
6. Does Mike have lunch in the school cafeteria? Yes, he has lunch in the school cafeteria.
7. Mike goes home at 3.30 p.m.
8. Mike doesn't play football in his school uniform.
9. Mike doesn't go home at 5.30 p.m.
10. Mike packs his school bag at 8.45 p.m.

Lösungen

11. Does Mike go to bed at 10.00 p.m.? No, he goes to bed at 9.00 p.m.

Seite 50/51

1 2. reading; 3. are drinking; 4. are playing; 5. is eating; 6. is buying; 7. is surfing; 8. are riding; 9. is selling; 10. are building; 11. is sitting

2
2. Who is reading a newspaper?
3. Who is playing volleyball?
4. Who is eating a banana?
5. Who is selling ice cream?
6. Who is surfing near the beach?

Seite 52

1
2. Hannah often takes out the rubbish.
3. Dad sometimes waters the plants. Oder: Dad waters the plants every Wednesday.
4. Mum and Dad never lay the table.
5. Josh sometimes feeds the cat. Oder: Josh feeds the cat every Thursday and Friday.
6. Mum cleans the living room every Friday.
7. Hannah makes breakfast every Wednesday.
8. Josh never goes shopping.

Seite 53

2 It's 8.15 a.m. Josh and Hannah are having (are eating) breakfast.
It's 8.30 a.m. Hannah is taking out the rubbish.
It's 4.30 p.m. Hannah is watering the plants.
It's 5.00 p.m. Mr Pott is making dinner.
It's 6.00 p.m. Josh is feeding the cat.

Seite 54/55 – Test

1
1. I've got (have got) a new school bag. It's (It is) red. My friend's (My friend is) in class 1C. Her parents are teachers.
2. There are twenty chairs and sixteen tables in our classroom. (In our classroom, there are ...) There are twelve boys and eleven girls in the class. There are four posters and a map of Great Britain on the wall. (On the wall, there are ...)
3. "Who's (is) Tom's aunt?"
"I don't (do not) know."
"But you are his friend."
"Yes. John and Peter are his brothers. And Fred is his uncle. But I don't (do not) know his aunt."
4. John always plays football on Saturdays. (On Saturdays, John ...) His sister often goes swimming with her friend. At the moment, John and his sister are doing something together. They are listening to music.

2 I play table tennis.
I don't (do not) play basketball.
Sarah plays the guitar. She (Sarah) doesn't (does not) watch TV.
Ben and Jamie go swimming. They (Ben and Jamie) don't (do not) play football.

3★
1. Where does Tom play football?
2. When does the school bus leave?
3. What does Mr Howard have for dinner on Fridays?
4. Why don't they have a picnic today?
5. How much coffee does Brenda's mother need?
6. Where does Mr Pott have lunch?
7. Why does Linda drink lemonade?
8. When does Josh do his homework?

Seite 56

1
2. I put my comics under the bed.
3. My books are on the bookshelf.
4. My school bag is under the desk.
5. I have got a chair, too.
6. My chair is in front of the desk.
7. A little lamp is next to my computer. Oder: Next to my computer is a little lamp.
8. I always put my shoes next to the desk.
9. I put the toy cars in a box.

Seite 57

2
① a book
② a school bag
③ a pillow
④ a mobile phone (cell phone)
⑤ an alarm clock
⑥ a poster

Seite 58

1
2. Jamie shows his father a new computer game.
3. Ben and Sarah buy their grandmother a present.
4. Mr Richards teaches the girls and boys English.
5. Susan tells her best friend Ann a secret.
6. The paperboy brings Mr Pott the newspaper.
7. Sarah and Jamie write their aunt Sally a letter.

Seite 59

2★
1. Peter lends his friend Ben a CD.
2. Susan writes her mother a postcard.
3. The teachers shows the pupils a new map.
4. When does Jamie buy his father a present?
5. Where do Mr and Mrs Pott buy their children new clothes?
6. When does Josh tell his sister a secret?
7. Why do Mr and Mrs Brown send the teacher a letter?
8. Grandma Brown tells her grandchildren a story.

Seite 60

1
Don't feed the animals.
Don't throw rubbish into the cages.
Don't lean over the walls.
Don't shout at the animals.

Seite 61

2
2. Feed the giraffes, but don't sit too close to them.
3. Close the crocodiles' door. Don't feed them.
4. Clean the bears' house. But don't eat or drink in the bears' house.
5. Play with the monkeys, but don't shout at them.

Seite 62 / 63 – Test

1
1. Don't (Do not) take photographs (photos).
2. Don't (Do not) eat ice cream.
3. Don't (Do not) play football.
4. Please don't (do not) smoke.

Lösungen

2 The Browns have got a garden. They are sitting under two trees. Mr Brown likes the summer because it's nice and warm. Look, a dog. It's Spooky, the Browns' dog. The dog always plays with Ben's shoes. Mrs Brown loves her flowers. Jamie and his sister's friend Tom don't like Mrs Brown's flowers: No football in the garden because of the flowers.

3
1. The boys are playing football this afternoon. Oder: This afternoon, the boys are playing football.
2. A dog is running after a cat.
3. Cats can run very fast.
4. There are no boats on the lake. Oder: On the lake there are no boats.
5. The park closes at 9.00 p.m. in summer. Oder: In summer, the park closes at 9.00 p.m.

4★
2. Cara Preedy is second, she often starts fast.
3. Colin Smith is third, he never talks to reporters.
4. Tom and Tim Johnson are fourth and fifth, they always finish together.

1 **Sieh dir den Stammbaum der Familie Brown genau an.**
Schreibe die richtige Form von *to be* in die Lücken der Aussagesätze.

Tipp: Die Liste auf Seite 28 hilft dir dabei.

1. Tom and Mary Brown ________ grandparents and Josh, Hannah, Ben, Jamie and Sarah ________ their grandchildren.
2. Mary: "Sally, Edmund and David ________ our children. Hannah ________ our granddaughter. And Sarah ________ our granddaughter, too. Josh, Ben and Jamie ________ our grandsons."
3. Robin Pott ________ Sally Pott's husband.
4. Josh Pott ________ Hannah Pott's brother.
5. Ben and Jamie Brown ________ brothers.
6. David: "I ________ Sally's and Edmund's brother. Linda ________ my wife." 11

2 **Schreibe die richtige Form von *to be* in die Lücken der Frage- und Antwortsätze.**

1. *Are* David and Linda Josh and Hannah's parents? No, they ________ not.
2. ________ Sally Edmund's wife? No, she ________ not, she ________ his sister.
3. ________ Ben Sarah's cousin? No, he ________ not. He ________ her brother.
4. Who ________ Hannah's aunt? Linda ________ her aunt. Edmund and David ________ her uncles.
5. What ________ the names of Sarah's parents? David and Linda.
6. Who ________ David and Linda's nephew? Josh ________ their nephew. 13

24–19 Punkte | 18–13 Punkte | 12–0 Punkte | Gesamtpunktzahl

simple present – Aussagesätze

Mit dem *simple present* drückt man Dinge aus, die immer (*always*) so sind oder die man regelmäßig immer wieder so macht. Das *simple present* hat dieselbe Form wie der Infinitiv, nur in der 3. Person Singular (*he, she* oder *it*) wird ein *-s* angehängt. Zum Beispiel *to sing* – singen: *I sing, you sing, they sing. We all sing together. But he always sings alone.*

1 **Welches Hobby passt zu welchem Verb? Trage die folgenden Hobbys in die Tabelle ein.**

swimming *the radio* *football* *action figures* *baseball cards*
music *ice-skating* *fishing* *model planes* *magazines*
the guitar *computer games* *TV* *a book* *comics*

to go	*swimming,*
to make	
to collect	*action figures,*
to play	
to listen to	
to read	
to watch	

13

Achtung: Im Deutschen heißt es „das Hobby" – „die Hobbys".
Im Englischen lautet der Plural jedoch *hobbies*.

2 **Daniel und seine Schwester Emma sprechen über ihre Hobbys. Lies die Sätze und schreibe dann einen Text über Daniel und Emma.**

Daniel: "Hi, I'm Daniel. I play football every afternoon. In the evening I always watch TV. At the weekend I sometimes go fishing with my friends. I make model planes, too."
Daniel and Emma: "Sometimes we do things together. We collect action figures and play computer games. In the evening we often listen to music or read a book."
Emma: "I always play hockey in the afternoon. I play the guitar, too. On Sundays I often go swimming with my friend Sandra. I never play football. I hate it."

Daniel plays football every afternoon.

pro richtigem Satz 1 Punkt | 11

24–19 Punkte | 18–13 Punkte | 12–0 Punkte | Gesamtpunktzahl

simple present – Verneinungen

Bei der Verneinung mit *to do* gibt es eine lange Form (*long form*) und eine kurze Form (*short form*):

Aussage	Verneinung – lange Form	Verneinung – kurze Form
I do	I do not	I don't
you do	you do not	you don't
he / she / it does	he / she / it does not	he / she / it doesn't
we do	we do not	we don't
you do	you do not	you don't
they do	they do not	they don't

Beispiele: *I play football. I don't play tennis.*
She plays volleyball. She doesn't play hockey.

Übrigens: *To be* wird ohne *to do* einfach mit *not* verneint:
I am here. I'm here. I am not here. I'm not here.
Nick is here. Nick's here. Tom is not here. Tom's not here.
They are here. They're here. They are not here. They're not here.

1 Lisa und Dylan haben beschlossen, den ganzen Tag zu faulenzen. Hier siehst du eine Liste mit den Dingen, die sie nicht tun. Lies die Liste und schreibe dann auf die Linien, was Lisa und Dylan alles nicht tun. Benutze die kurze Form der Verneinung.

Lisa: to take the dog for a walk
to play table tennis in the park
to go to the sports club
to work in the garden
to read a magazine

Dylan: to go swimming
to go fishing in the river
to ride his bike
to play football
to visit Grandma

Lisa doesn't take the dog for a walk. ______________________________

She ______________________________

____

____

____

Dylan

9

2 Dylan hat in einer E-Mail an seinen Freund Ben ganz schön geflunkert. Schreibe die E-Mail neu und verneine dabei jeden Satz. Benutze die lange Form der Verneinung.

```
Dear Ben,
Today we are very busy*. My sister Lisa is in the garden.
She and my mother like gardening. My brother Alan is on a
bike ride. On Sundays I go fishing with my friend Bob.
I often go fishing. The weather is fine. Lisa takes our
dog for a walk every afternoon. We have a lot to do
today.
Love, Dylan
```

* *busy* = beschäftigt

Dear Ben,
Today we are not very busy.

pro verneintem Verb 1 Punkt 8

17–14 Punkte | 13–9 Punkte | 8–0 Punkte | Gesamtpunktzahl

simple present – Fragesätze

1 **Jeden Tag um 8 Uhr schaut Mrs Smith aus dem Fenster, und jeden Tag sieht sie das Gleiche. Schau dir das Bild genau an. Lies dann die Antworten (A für *answer*). Schreibe zu jeder Antwort die richtige Frage (Q für *question*) auf. Ergänze auch die Antworten, wo es nötig ist.**

1. Q: *Does the man in the brown coat go to work by car?*

   A: No, the man in the brown coat doesn't go to work by car.

   He goes to work by bus.

2. Q: Are ____________________?

   A: Yes, the traffic lights are red for the bus every morning at eight o'clock.

3. Q: Does ____________________ every morning?

   A: Yes, the cat runs after the dog every morning.

4. Q: Who ____________________?

   A: The policeman talks to reckless drivers* every morning.

* *reckless drivers* = rücksichtslose Autofahrer

5. Q: ____?

A: No, the postman never stops at number 34.

But he always ______________________________________ 32.

6. Q: ____?

A: Yes, the boys go to school on their rollerblades.

7. Q: ____?

A: No, bus number 4 doesn't go to Portobello.

It ____.

8. Q: ____?

A: No, the girl doesn't look in the window of the toy shop every morning.

She ____. ___ 10

10–8 Punkte | 7–5 Punkte | 4–0 Punkte | Gesamtpunktzahl

simple present – Fragewörter

Fragewörter (*question words*) leiten einen Fragesatz ein.

Fragewort	Bedeutung
What?	Was?
When?	Wann?
Where?	Wo?
Why?	Warum?

1 In den Klammern stehen Antworten auf Fragen. Formuliere mithilfe der angegebenen Satzteile die entsprechenden Fragen. Benutze dazu die richtige Form von *to do* und die Fragewörter aus dem Merkkasten. Schreibe die Antworten in ganzen Sätzen unter die Fragen.

1. Mrs Brown / to buy / a newspaper (in the morning)
   When does Mrs Brown buy a newspaper?
   She buys a newspaper in the morning.

2. Jack / to buy / chocolate bars (because he is hungry)

______________________________?

______________________________.

3. Vicky / to buy / magazines (at the kiosk)

______________________________?

______________________________.

4. Julia and Tim / to buy (bread and ten eggs)

______________________________?

______________________________.

5. Mrs Solomon / to buy (a packet of cornflakes and two bottles of milk)

____ ?

____ .

6. Ben and Jamie / to buy / a comic (because they want to read it)

____ ?

____ .

7. Mr Smart / to buy (a book)

____ ?

____ .

8. Lisa / to buy / a new T-shirt (on Monday)

____ ?

____ .

9. Hannah / to buy / three bottles of apple juice (at the supermarket)

____ ?

____ .

10. Mr Pott / to buy / a new bicycle (on Saturday)

____ ?

____ . ☐ 18

 ☐ 18–15 Punkte | 14–10 Punkte | 9–0 Punkte | ☐ Gesamtpunktzahl

simple present – Kurzformen

1 **Du gehst mit Sarah und Jamie in ein Restaurant.**
Lies die Unterhaltung und schreibe die passenden Kurzformen in die Lücken. Streiche die Kurzformen durch, die du schon benutzt hast.

Don't don't don't haven't He's here's ~~I'm~~ I'm I'm
It's it's Let's let's That's ~~that's~~ that's ~~They've~~ you're

Jamie: "__________ hungry."

You: "*I'm* glad that __________ hungry. __________ hungry, too."

Sarah: "__________ go into that restaurant over there."

You: "Good idea. __________ my favourite restaurant."

Sarah: "I hope __________ not an expensive restaurant. I __________ got much money."

You: "__________ worry. We __________ want anything expensive. Look, __________ the waiter. __________ very nice."

Waiter: "Good afternoon. Can I help you?"

You: "Can we have the menu*, please?"

Waiter: "Here you are."

You: "OK, __________ see. *They've* got a big plate of chips for £ 1.50 or a small plate for £ 1."

Sarah: "How much is a lemonade?"

Waiter: "__________ 80 p."

Sarah: "I want a lemonade and a small plate of chips, please."

You: "Me, too."

Jamie: "Yes, ______________ a good idea. Me too, please."

Waiter: "So, *that's* three lemonades and three small plates of chips."

You: "What about ketchup? Can we have ketchup on our chips?"

Waiter: "Yes, of course."

Jamie: "I ______________ like ketchup. No ketchup for me, please." ___ | 15

* *the menu* = die Speisekarte

2 **Nur einer der folgenden Texte mit Langformen ist richtig. Lies die beiden Texte und kreuze den richtigen an.**

☐ **A** My parents and I do not like that snack-bar because the waiter is not very friendly. He has old and he has got a dog called Annie. She is black and she is got a very big mouth. My father does not want me to play with her. He has not happy with dogs.

☐ **B** My parents and I do not like that snack-bar because the waiter is not very friendly. He is old and he has got a dog called Annie. She is black and she has got a very big mouth. My father does not want me to play with her. He is not happy with dogs. ___ | 1

3 **Schreibe den richtigen Text auf die Linien und wandele dabei alle Langformen in Kurzformen um.**

My parents and I don't like ______________________________

____

____

____

____

____ ___ | 7

☐ 23–19 Punkte 18–13 Punkte 12–0 Punkte ☐ Gesamtpunktzahl

1 **Mike hat aufgeschrieben, was er jeden Tag macht. Lies seinen Zeitplan. Bilde dann mit den angegebenen Satzteilen Aussagesätze (✓), Verneinungen (✗) oder Fragen (?). Schreibe zu den Fragen auch die Antworten in ganzen Sätzen.**

7.00 a.m.	*get up and wash*
7.15 a.m.	*put on school uniform*
7.30 a.m.	*have breakfast*
8.20 a.m.	*brush teeth and comb hair*
8.30 a.m.	*leave the house and catch the bus*
9.00 a.m.	*school starts*
12.30 a.m.	*have lunch in the school cafeteria*
1.15 p.m.	*school starts again*
3.30 p.m.	*go home*
4.00 p.m.	*get home and get changed**
4.10 p.m.	*meet my friends in the park for a game of football*
6.00 p.m.	*go home for tea***
7.10 p.m.	*meet my friends in the park for another game of football*
8.30 p.m.	*go home*
8.45 p.m.	*pack my school bag for the next day*
8.50 p.m.	*wash and brush teeth*
9.00 p.m.	*go to bed*

* *to get changed* = sich umziehen
** *tea* bedeutet hier Abendessen

1. Mike / to get up / 7.00 a.m. (✓)
   Mike gets up at 7.00 a.m.

2. Mike / to put on school uniform / 7.15 a.m. (?)

   Does Mike ______________ *his* ______________ *at 7.15 a.m.?*

Yes, he puts on ______________________.

3. Mike / to leave the house / 8.30 a.m. (✓)

____

4. school / to start / 8.00 a.m. (?) ______________________

____

5. Mike / to have lunch / at 1.00 p.m. (✗)

____

6. Mike / to have lunch / in the school cafeteria (?) ______________________

____

7. Mike / to go home / 3.30 p.m. (✓)

____

8. Mike / to play football / in his school uniform (✗)

____

9. Mike / to go home / 5.30 p.m. (✗)

____

10. Mike / to pack school bag / 8.45 p.m. (✓)

____

11. Mike / to go to bed / 10.00 p.m. (?) ______________________

____

______________________ [ ] 14

14–11 Punkte

10–8 Punkte

7–0 Punkte

Gesamtpunktzahl

Das *present progressive* (auch *present continuous* genannt) beschreibt, was jetzt gerade geschieht.
Es steht deshalb oft zusammen mit Ausdrücken wie *at the moment, now* oder *at present*. Es wird gebildet mit *am / is / are* und der *-ing*-Form des Verbs:
I am reading a book at the moment.

1 **Sieh dir das Bild genau an. Schreibe dann auf, was die Menschen am Strand gerade tun. Die angegebenen Verben helfen dir dabei.**

1. *Some children are swimming in the sea.*

2. A man in shorts is ______________________ a newspaper.

3. Two girls ______________________ lemonade.

4. Three girls and three boys ______________________ volleyball.

5. A small child ______________________ a banana.

6. A boy ______________________ an ice cream.

7. A young woman ______________________ near the beach.

8. A boy and a girl ______________________ their mountain bikes.

9. A young man ______________________ ice cream.

10. An old lady and her grandchild ______________________ a sandcastle.

11. A girl ______________________ on the sand. ___ /10

2 **Bilde zu den Antworten die richtigen Fragen im *present progressive*.**

1. *Who is swimming in the sea?* Some children are swimming in the sea.

2. Who is ______________________ a newspaper? A man in shorts.

3. Who ______________________? Three girls and three boys.

4. Who ______________________ a banana? A small child.

5. Who ______________________ ice cream? A young man.

6. Who ______________________ near the beach? A young woman. ___ /5

15–12 Punkte | 11–8 Punkte | 7–0 Punkte | Gesamtpunktzahl

Mit diesen Zeitangaben stehen Verben sehr oft im *simple present*:

usually	normalerweise
always	immer
never	nie
often	oft
sometimes	manchmal
every Monday (Tuesday ...)	jeden Montag (Dienstag ...)

1 Hier siehst du den Aufgabenplan der Familie Pott. Schreibe im *simple present* auf die Linien, welche Aufgaben jedes Familienmitglied nie, manchmal, oft, jeden Montag (Dienstag ...) oder immer erledigt. Benutze die Angaben in den Klammern.

jobs	Monday	Tuesday	Wednesday	Thursday	Friday	weekend
lay the table	Josh	Josh	Josh	Josh	Josh	Josh
make breakfast	Mum	Mum	Hannah	Mum	Mum	Dad
take out the rubbish	Hannah	Hannah	Hannah	Hannah	Hannah	Josh
make dinner	Mum	Mum	Mum	Dad	Dad	Mum
go shopping	Mum	Mum	Mum	Hannah	Hannah	–
water the plants	Josh	–	Dad	–	Hannah	–
clean the living room	Dad	Dad	Hannah	Josh	Mum	–
feed the cat	Hannah	Hannah	Hannah	Josh	Josh	Mum

1. (the table) Josh *always lays the table.*
2. (the rubbish) Hannah ______________________
3. (the plants) Dad ______________________
4. (the table) Mum and Dad ______________________
5. (the cat) Josh ______________________

6. (the living room) Mum ....

7. (breakfast) Hannah ....

8. (shopping) Josh 7

2 **Sieh dir die Bilder an und schreibe auf, was die Mitglieder der Familie Pott zu bestimmten Uhrzeiten gerade tun. Verwende das *present progressive*.**

Tipp: Wenn du nicht mehr weißt, wie das *present progressive* gebildet wird, blättere einfach eine Seite zurück (S. 50).

It's 8 o'clock a.m. Mrs Pott is making breakfast.

It's 8.15 a.m. Josh and Hannah ....

It's ....

It's ....

It's ....

It's 5

12–10 Punkte | 9–7 Punkte | 6–0 Punkte | Gesamtpunktzahl

simple present / present progressive

Mit diesem Test kannst du überprüfen, was du schon kannst.
Tipp: Wenn du Schwierigkeiten hast, schau auf den angegebenen Seiten nach.

1 Schreibe die folgenden Sätze auf Englisch auf ein Blatt Papier.

1. Ich habe eine neue Schultasche. Sie ist rot. Meine Freundin ist in Klasse 1C. Ihre Eltern sind Lehrer. (Seite 14–15)

2. In unserem Klassenraum sind zwanzig Stühle und sechzehn Tische. Es sind zwölf Jungen und elf Mädchen in der Klasse. An den Wänden sind vier Poster und eine Karte von Großbritannien. (Seite 4–5)

3. „Wer ist Toms Tante?" „Ich weiß es nicht." „Aber du bist sein Freund." „Ja. John und Peter sind seine Brüder. Und Fred ist sein Onkel. Aber ich kenne seine Tante nicht." (Seite 16–17, 28, 37, 40–41)

4. John spielt am Samstag immer Fußball. Seine Schwester geht oft mit ihrer Freundin schwimmen. Im Moment machen John und seine Schwester etwas zusammen. Sie hören Musik. (Seite 38–39, 50–51) ____ /17

2 Schau dir die Tabelle an und schreibe drei Aussagesätze (✓) und drei verneinte Sätze (✗) auf die Linien. (Seite 38–41)

	✓	✗
I	to play table tennis	to play basketball
Sarah	to play the guitar	to watch TV
Ben and Jamie	to go swimming	to play football

____

____

____

____

____

____ 6

3 Die Sätze 1–8 sind Antworten auf Fragen. Schreibe über jeden Satz die richtige Frage. Die Fragewörter sind vorgegeben. (Seite 44–45)

Where ____?
1. Tom plays football in the park.

When ____?
2. The school bus leaves at 8.30 a.m.

What ____?
3. Mr Howard has fish for dinner on Fridays.

Why ____?
4. They don't have a picnic today because it's raining.

How much ____?
5. Brenda's mother needs a pound of coffee.

Where ____?
6. Mr Pott has lunch at the cafeteria.

Why ____?
7. Linda drinks lemonade because she's thirsty.

When ____?
8. Josh does his homework in the evening.

pro richtiger Frage 2 Punkte 16

39–33 Punkte | 32–20 Punkte | 19–0 Punkte | Gesamtpunktzahl

Wortstellung (1)

Die Wortstellung (*word order*) in englischen Aussagesätzen ist festgelegt:

Subjekt	Prädikat	Objekt
I	*read*	*a book.*

Adverbien des Ortes stehen am Satzende.

Subjekt	Prädikat	Objekt	Adverb des Ortes
I	*have got*	*a computer*	*on my desk.*

1 Die folgenden Sätze sind genauso durcheinander wie Bens Zimmer. Bringe die Satzteile in die richtige Reihenfolge.

1. (a computer) (I) (have got) (on my desk) *I have got a computer on my desk.*

2. (I) (under the bed) (put) (my comics)

   ....

3. (are) (my books) (on the bookshelf)

   ....

4. (is) (under the desk) (my school bag)

____

5. (have got) (a chair) (too) (I)

____

6. (in front of) (the desk) (is) (my chair)

____

7. (next to) (my computer) (a little lamp) (is)

____

8. (always) (I) (next to) (the desk) (my shoes) (put)

____

9. (the toy cars) (in a box) (I) (put)

____ __ / 8

2 Sechs Gegenstände in Bens Zimmer sind nummeriert. Schreibe auf, wie sie auf Englisch heißen.

Tipp: Wenn du ein Wort nicht weißt, schlag in einem Wörterbuch nach.

① ________________ ② ________________

③ ________________ ④ ________________

⑤ ________________ ⑥ ________________ __ / 6

14–12 Punkte | 11–8 Punkte | 7–0 Punkte | Gesamtpunktzahl

Wortstellung (2)

Ein Verb kann im Satz zwei Objekte haben. Das direkte Objekt (*direct object*) bezeichnet meist Sachen, das indirekte Objekt (*indirect object*) meist Personen.

Die Person steht in der Regel vor der Sache.

Subjekt	Prädikat	indirektes Objekt	direktes Objekt
He	*gives*	*her*	*a book.*

1 Bringe die folgenden Subjekte, Prädikate und Objekte in die richtige Reihenfolge. Schreibe ganze Sätze auf die Linien.

1. sends / Hannah / a postcard / her friend Emma

   Hannah sends her friend Emma a postcard.

2. Jamie / his father / shows / a new computer game

   ____

3. buy / Ben and Sarah / their grandmother / a present

   ____

4. the girls and boys / English / teaches / Mr Richards

   ____

5. tells / Susan / a secret / her best friend Ann

   ____

6. the newspaper / brings / Mr Pott / the paperboy

   ____

7. their aunt Sally / write / a letter / Sarah and Jamie

   ______________________________ | | 6 |

2 **Schreibe die folgenden Sätze in Englisch auf die Linien. Denke bei Fragen an die richtige Form von *to do*.**

Tipp: Die Fragewörter findest du auf Seite 44.

1. Peter leiht* seinem Freund Ben eine CD.

____

2. Susan schreibt ihrer Mutter eine Postkarte.

____

3. Der Lehrer zeigt den Schülern eine neue Landkarte.

____

4. Wann kauft Jamie seinem Vater ein Geschenk?

____

5. Wo kaufen Mr und Mrs Pott ihren Kindern neue Kleidungsstücke**?

____

6. Wann erzählt Josh seiner Schwester ein Geheimnis?

____

7. Warum schicken Mr und Mrs Brown dem Lehrer einen Brief?

____

8. Großmutter Brown erzählt ihren Enkeln eine Geschichte.

____ [ ] 8

* leihen = *to lend*
** Kleidungsstücke = *clothes*

[ ] 14–12 Punkte | 11–8 Punkte | 7–0 Punkte | [ ] Gesamtpunktzahl

Aufforderungen

Eine Aufforderung (*command*) heißt auch Imperativ. Sie sieht im Englischen genauso aus wie der Infinitiv, aber ohne *to*.
Ein Beispiel: Infinitiv: *to drive* – fahren; Aufforderung: *Drive.* – Fahr los!
Eine verneinte Aufforderung (ein Verbot) wird mit *do not* oder *don't* gebildet: *Don't drive.* – Fahr nicht!

1 **Im Zoo gibt es einige Dinge, die Besucher nicht tun sollten. Sieh dir die Schilder an und schreibe unter jedes Schild eine verneinte Aufforderung. Die Wörter neben den Bildern helfen dir.**

take photos

Don't take photos here ______________________

feed the animals

____

throw rubbish into the cages

____

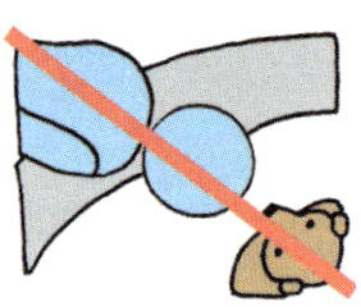

lean over the walls

____

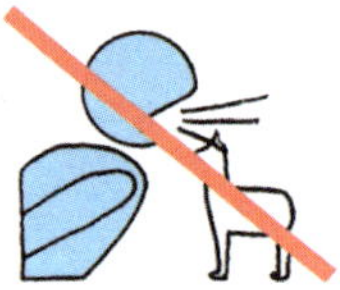

shout at the animals

____

[   ] 4

2 **Ann arbeitet seit heute im Zoo. Der Tierpfleger sagt ihr, was sie tun soll und was sie nicht tun soll. Lies seine Anweisungen und schreibe sie dann auf Englisch auf. Die folgenden Wörter helfen dir.**

clean *shout at* *feed* *open* *run* *sit* *close* *play* *eat or drink*
elephants' house *the crocodiles' door* *too close to them* *the bears' house*
the giraffes *the monkeys*

1. Sie soll das Elefantenhaus öffnen, aber nicht in das Elefantenhaus hineinrennen.
   Open the elephants' house. But don't run into it.

2. Sie soll die Giraffen füttern, aber sie soll nicht zu nah bei ihnen sitzen.

   ______________________________ ,

   but ______________________________ .

3. Sie soll die Tür der Krokodile schließen. Sie soll die Krokodile nicht füttern.

   ______________________________ .

   ______________________________ .

4. Sie soll das Bärenhaus sauber machen. Sie soll aber nicht im Bärenhaus essen oder trinken.

   ______________________________ .

   ______________________________ .

5. Sie soll mit den Affen spielen, sie soll sie aber nicht anschreien.

   ______________________________ ,

   ______________________________ . ☐ 8

☐ 12–10 Punkte 9–7 Punkte 6–0 Punkte ☐ Gesamtpunktzahl

Wortstellung / Aufforderungen

Mit diesem Test kannst du überprüfen, was du schon kannst.
Tipp: Wenn du Schwierigkeiten hast, schau auf den angegebenen Seiten nach.

1 Schreibe die folgenden Aufforderungen in Englisch auf die Linien. (Seite 60–61)

1. Nicht fotografieren. ____________________
2. Kein Eis essen. ____________________
3. Fußball spielen verboten. ____________________
4. Bitte nicht rauchen*. ____________________

__ | 4

* rauchen = *to smoke*

2 Schreibe jeweils die richtige Endung (-*s*, *'s* oder *s'*) auf die Linien. (Seite 8–13)

The Brown___ have got a garden. They are sitting under two tree___.

Mr Brown like___ the summer because it___ nice and warm. Look, a dog.

It___ Spooky, the Brown___ dog. The dog always play___ with Ben___ shoe___.

Mrs Brown love___ her flower___. Jamie and his sister___ friend Tom don't

like Mrs Brown___ flower___: No football in the garden because of the

flower___.

__ | 15

3 Bilde aus den folgenden Wörtern ganze Sätze. Achte auf die Wortstellung. (Seite 56–59)

1. playing / football / this afternoon / are / the boys

2. after a cat / is / a dog / running

3. run / cats / can / fast / very

4. boats / on / there are / the lake / no

5. closes / the park / at 9.00 p.m. / in summer

5

4 Hier siehst du, wer bei einem Marathonlauf die ersten fünf Plätze belegt hat. Bilde mit den Angaben in der Tabelle drei vollständige Sätze. (Seite 38–39, 52)

place	notes
1st: Wang Fu	always fast (to run)
2nd: Cara Preedy	often fast (to start)
3rd: Colin Smith	never to reporters (to talk)
4th and 5th: Tom and Tim Johnson	always together (to finish)

1. *Wang Fu is first, he always runs fast.*
2.
3.
4.

6

30–25 Punkte

24–16 Punkte

15–0 Punkte

Gesamtpunktzahl

Autorinnen: Ingrid Preedy und Brigitte Seidl

www.cornelsen.de

Bibliografische Information:
Die Deutsche Bibliothek verzeichnet diese Publikation in der Deutschen Nationalbibliografie; detaillierte bibliografische Daten sind im Internet über http://dnb.ddb.de abrufbar.

Dieser Band folgt den Regeln der deutschen Rechtschreibung, die seit August 2006 gelten.

5. 4. 3. 2. 1. Die letzten Ziffern bezeichnen
13 12 11 10 09 Zahl und Jahr der Auflage.

Projektleitung: Annegret Hauser, Berlin
Redaktion: lüra – Klemt & Mues GbR, Wuppertal
Reihengestaltung: Magdalene Krumbeck, Wuppertal
Satz und Layout: Ludger Stallmeister, Wuppertal
Illustrationen: Dorina Teßmann, Berlin
Umschlagentwurf: Magdalene Krumbeck, Wuppertal
Druck und Bindearbeiten: Saaledruck Naumburg GmbH
Printed in Germany
ISBN 978-3-589-22792-1

Gedruckt auf säurefreiem Papier,
umweltschonend hergestellt aus chlorfrei gebleichten Faserstoffen.